Dream Big for Addison

Les Bookman

E-Book: 978-1-969066-02-3
Paperback: 978-1-969066-00-9
Hardcover: 978-1-969066-01-6

Published by
Columbus Book Publishers
www.columbusbookpublishers.com

Printed in the United States of America

Dedication

I dedicate this book to my granddaughter Addison Bluu Bookman, she is the inspiration for this book because she really dreams about being more than one thing in life at a young age. Addison is truly a great soul to enjoy and be around all day, every day. The entire family loves you, Addison!

About the Author

Hello, my name is Les Bookman and I am the grandfather of Addison. Kids are our inspiration and I am trying to be a great author to show my granddaughter that you can achieve whatever it is that you want to do in life.

On One fine day, Addison was sitting in a bright, colorful classroom with her friends.

The teacher standing in front said, "Today, we're going to talk about our dreams! What do you want to be when you grow up?"

Dreams

Addison's eyes sparkled. She wanted to tell her dream!

"Lucas," asked Mr. Brown, "what's your dream?"

Lucas grinned. "I want to be a pilot! I'll fly planes across the sky!"

The class cheered.

"Whoosh!" said Addison, zooming her hands like an airplane.

"I also want to fly, but in Space! I want to be an astronaut!" Addison exclaimed.

Mr. Brown smiled and nodded.

"That's a wonderful dream, Addison," he said. "Why do you want to be an astronaut?"

Addison grinned, "I want to discover new things and explore the unknown, I want to go on big adventures and see things no one else has seen before!"

Addison's friends cheered and clapped for her in amazement.

During recess, the children ran outside, buzzing with excitement. Sophia sat under a tree, drawing. "I want to be an artist," she said. "I'll paint the whole world beautiful!"

Noah kicked a soccer ball. "I want to be a pro athlete!" he said. "I'll win trophies"

Addison watched her friends, her heart full of dreams.

Back in class, Mr. Brown turned to Sarah "What do you want to be, when you grow up Sarah?"

"I want to be a singer!" Sarah said. "I love to sing and make people happy."

"Ooo and I love to write, I would like to be a writer too someday" Addison said, her voice filled with excitement. "I want to tell stories that inspire and entertain people."

"Hey, maybe we can write and sing together in a duo and become famous!" replied Sarah.

"Yes girls, that is a very nice dream," replied Mr. Brown.

Next, Mr. Brown turned to Emma. "How about you, Emma?"
Emma twirled. "I want to be a doctor! I'll help people feel strong and healthy again!"
Addison clapped. "You'll be an amazing doctor!

Mr. Brown then asked, "Does anyone have more dreams they'd like to share?"

"I also want to be a data scientist!" said Addison, raising her hand.

"I want to find hidden treasures in numbers and help solve big problems!"

"That's great Addison, it's a very nice dream," Mr. Brown replied.

"Or I would like to be a chef!" Addison added, her smile growing wider. "I love eating delicious food and I would love to make tasty dishes so people can enjoy my food."

"I would eat at your restaurant every day!!!" exclaimed lucas.

Addison smiled with pride.

Lastly, Mr. Brown asked Mia, “Mia, do you have dreams you would like to achieve?"

"I want to be an AI engineer!" Mia said excitedly.

"I want to create smart machines that can help people."

"Wow, that sounds amazing!" Addison said.
"We can all dream big and do amazing things, when we grow up!"
"Absolutely!" the teacher smiled. "No matter what you dream of being, remember to work hard, stay curious, and never give up. Your dreams are worth chasing!

Dreams

I have so many dreams
that could come true.

www.ingramcontent.com/pod-product-compliance
Lightning Source LLC
LaVergne TN
LVHW060411220926
848484LV00015B/2386

* 9 7 8 1 9 6 9 0 6 6 0 5 4 *